A TO Z OF LIVING FOR WOMEN

THE JOURNEY FROM SURVIVING TO THRIVING

SIMMI ROY MISHRA

AF518684

BlueRoseONE.com
Stories Matter
NewDelhi • London

BLUEROSE PUBLISHERS
India | U.K.

Copyright © Simmi Roy Mishra 2024

All rights reserved by author. No part of this publication may be reproduced, stored in a retrieval system or transmitted in any form or by any means, electronic, mechanical, photocopying, recording or otherwise, without the prior permission of the author. Although every precaution has been taken to verify the accuracy of the information contained herein, the publisher assumes no responsibility for any errors or omissions. No liability is assumed for damages that may result from the use of information contained within.

BlueRose Publishers takes no responsibility for any damages, losses, or liabilities that may arise from the use or misuse of the information, products, or services provided in this publication.

For permissions requests or inquiries regarding this publication, please contact:

BLUEROSE PUBLISHERS
www.BlueRoseONE.com
info@bluerosepublishers.com
+91 8882 898 898
+4407342408967

ISBN: 978-93-5989-720-2

Cover Design: Sadhna Kumari
Typesetting: Pooja Sharma

First Edition: April 2024

This book is dedicated to

all the women who went missing,

From the wombs and the cradles,

From homes and the schools,

From the colleges and workplaces,

From relationships

Because

Some were not allowed to live while some were not taught,

Some did not know where to live while some did not know why,

Some wondered when to live while some simply forgot how,

And then some were questioned about the way,

They chose to live.

Acknowledgements

I thank Papa for always believing in me, Maa for choosing to thrive, my brother, Roshan, for his support, my husband, Rakesh, for being a lovely partner, Mummyji for her blessings, sister-in-law Tanuja for being a cheerleader, my daughters, Anahita and Anushka, for their delightful presence in my life.

I am surrounded and loved by a tribe of formidable women - Winnie, Pushpa, Samiksha, Priyanka, Ekta and Kalpa.

I am full of gratitude to Miss Felicia, my teachers, and mentors.

And above all a big thank you to the women I treated as patients and coached as clients over the years

Contents

Aware

Know Who You Are

Each of us experiences restlessness at some level. For some, it worsens and surfaces as anxiety, while for others, it manifests as overthinking. Eventually, it has the potential to take a toll on our well-being. So, where and why does this restlessness arise? The most common reasons include unaligned thoughts and actions, shifting goalposts, comparison among peers, societal pressure, and self-beliefs.

The truth is, we are often woefully unaware of our own selves. It is crucial to be conscious of our values, beliefs, strengths, goals, skills, and resources. Life need not be chaotic; it need not be a race. Life is meant to be lived with joy.

Dedicate time, again and again, to being truly aware of who you are. Once you genuinely discover yourself, that marks the beginning of peace.

Begin

Where You Are, With What You Have

The most difficult part of life for women is the beginning. the home they are born in, school, new workplace, after marriage, motherhood or going back to work. It's overwhelming, isn't it?

The journey to betterment and excellence, one remains still in incertitude many times. It is disheartening to experience blocks, rejections, and doubt by self and others, being constantly judged and no wonder many succumb and few rise.

The ones who make it to the top are those who simply begin by taking one day a time.

Trust Yourself. Because no one's will until you trust your own self. There will always be voices. Are you sure? Do you really want to do it? So, the only thing that will keep you going is trusting yourself round the clock.

Kickstart everyday with a routine. The journey ahead is long and arduous.

Nourishing your body and mind with a beautiful routine of meditation and exercises helps in more than one way. It regulates neurotransmitters that rule your thoughts.

Set standards for what you stand for. You are your own brand and brand ambassador. And never let go of at any time. And just live up to it as much as possible through the journey.

We are all here to showcase who we are.

And in our eyes lie dreams of glory and recognition. Be ready for it all by beginning in the right way.

Celebrate

Every Small Win

We all have heard the word "triggers". A **trigger** is a person, place, thing, or situation that elicits an intense or unexpected emotional response.

It brings about a deep sense of discomfort and even despair. But have you heard of glimmers. These are exactly the opposite of triggers. While everyone is aware of the latter, the former is barely known.

Glimmers are tiny moments of happiness that bring an intense sense of joy, awe or delight. Just as we feel low or angry when triggered, tune into little celebrations when you experience glimmers.

No matter where you are, look around every day. The sky, the clouds, the trees, the breeze, the sun... well almost everything. Each has the power to anchor your moments of joy. Celebrate the ability to experience it.

Next focus on your own life. Stir in the direction from despair to calm by being mindful of your thoughts. At every given point in life there is something to be positive about. You need to stir to look at it. Every little win is to be celebrated. We often choose to acknowledge bigger achievements.

Remember how the tennis players celebrate every point! Well, that's exactly what a glimmer looks like!

In the end it's a choice.

Open your mind to glimmers instead of triggers and watch yourself transform.

In the beginning it takes some effort and later on it's a routine in life.

Discover

Little Things about Yourself

We all need to discover little things about ourselves - You are bigger than what you create or represent.

Anyone who reaches out to you is because of your own inherent style. Look around any product, it has over 100 options to choose from. In all possible budgets. And in lucrative packaging. But what makes one better than the other is the person associated with it. That's why brand ambassadors work and charge a bomb.

So, what about you?

Every place you stand and speak you will be watched very closely.

Your words, your pauses, the way you walk, stand and move, the way you eat, how you look, everything represents you.

So, discover your mannerisms, correct and modify them to help you personally and professionally.

Energize

Daily to Keep Going

"I am tired," said almost every woman to me.

"I am looking forward to a vacation but I guess it will only be worse," said another.

The only way to do away with tiredness is to energize yourself every day Self-care is an essential part of life. Burnout is real. While many factors contribute to it it's astonishing that every individual somehow contributes to his or her own suffering.

That's simply because while we were taught to bathe, clean, eat and exercise as a routine, nothing similar was outlined to us regarding the care of our minds.

It's heartbreaking to see people literally "lose" themselves a bit by bit everyday

Energize by taking breaks every day. Prioritize eating, exercise, walks, meditations and spending time with nature to energize yourself. Our body and mind need care on a daily basis. Not just once in a while. We need to put in at least 30 mins to this, begin with 5 mins at least.

Listen to the needs of your body and mind and when you do that you will know how to choose yourself over and over again. When we choose

ourselves we set the tone of how others treat us. Never forget that!

Filter

What Reaches Your Mind

Almost any and every thought can find a place in your mind. It can make or break you

But do you know that ... "Thoughts become things"

So, make a conscious choice to filter what you listen to

While you're thinking depends on your own perceptions it can also be deeply influenced by what you hear.

Make connections with the right people. Who we surround ourselves with is one the most powerful investments. Good minds are gold mines of right thoughts. The words they utter can provoke your thinking and generate ideas that change you and your life!

Avoid all kinds of negative news, social media and even people. Social media invariably consumes our mind. One news can trigger thoughts that do not serve you in any way. It does have potential to shift your focus and energy tremendously

Go old school by choosing to read rather than scroll.

Trust me it's a very simple way to filter what reaches your mind.

Grow

Through What You Go Through

Drowned in the pain of challenges are the lessons for life. If we pick those soaked in blood and tears, dry them in the light of success and read them aloud after we have triumphed, we find treasures that can serve us and others in the life that lies ahead.

Every situation gives us victory or learning.

And while victory is personal it's the learning that can serve the people around you and society at large

Because the truth is if we keep ourselves open to learning we actually grow through the situations

Always choose to respond rather than react. Every situation, to every person and every time. In our response lies the path to betterment. In reactions lie the seeds of trouble and pain. Our response is watched by everyone and that learning is one the most powerful ones.

History tells us stories about successful people. Each of them turned the challenge into opportunity. It applies to all of us. Make the best of it. And watch your self-etching history of your own!! It's better to shine than whine any day!

You are worthy and deserving of all love, respect and success. It may be trying, and difficult at times painful but the ability to hang on, show up and learn.

Heal

On a Regular Basis

Well, the truth is, accumulated hurt leads to what is known as chronic post-traumatic stress disorder which can make the healing and recovery longer and at times very difficult.

We often associate trauma with something really big like death of loved one, disability or disease, financial loss and separation

But did you know there can be day to day traumas that are subtle, harmful and can eventually feel worse after varying periods of time.

Emotional abuse, verbal abuse, harassment at workplace, constant gaslighting, disrespect and lack of inclusion. All this have the potential to be accumulative as we fail to recognise them.

But the onus lies completely on US

Make time to acknowledge your pain and HEAL

Hold on to yourself, not the situation. You are more important than anything else. Embrace your values and peace. And while you do this assess if the trauma you are going through is actually repetitive or not.

Have courage to step away from values that don't serve you or make life difficult. Many times, people simply take advantage of who you are. And you keep sticking to your own image

Learning the art of letting go is a daily ritual not once in a lifetime act. If you learn this art, every day will be worthwhile. Pray, meditate, be with your tribe... take your pick but do it

It doesn't matter who or what hurts but it does matter that You heal

I

Intention

Should be Set Everyday

Intention precedes action and determines a lot that unfolds in our lives. Very often we are engrossed in results that a certain act will bring rather than focussing on the intent driving the act. That's exactly where all the mistakes lie.

Your intent comes from the values you are rooted to. And it can make you stand out in the crowd. The same act may be performed by a group of people but it's the intent that separates one from another

Intention reminds you of your purpose constantly. If you are contributing to greater good and giving value it drives you even during challenging times Your skills, talents, strengths are all in use when your intention is right. It

helps in self-realization and self-discovery and turn things in your favor.

Because the intention set by you is known to the universe. And that energy is so powerful!

It has the power to create magic

So be it for life, decade, year, month, week or day Focus on intention.

The act and results will simply follow

J

Jest

Because Joy is Your True State

Laughter certainly is a medicine from the body's very own pharmacy! A good laugh can

Boosts mood Diminishes pain Establishes connect fosters relationships

It also protects and strengthens the immune system.

Do you remember how you laughed when you were little? And how many times do you laugh now?

It's disheartening that we actually stop laughing as we grow up. Make a point to find ways to laugh every day

Interact with kids Watch sitcoms Crack jokes

Or read funny books

But make a conscious attempt

Let your body and mind soak into endorphins!! To begin with

Smile generously whole day

Be grateful and express gratitude Bring a dash of humor at workplace

Make it a conscious practice and reap benefits

Don't forget every laugh will take you to a place in the world that looks much happier than it actually is!!

Kindle

Your Own Fire and Light Your Own Path

Each of us has inherent potential — the potential to transform and move into roles that life demands of us, the potential to undertake varied challenges that it throws at us, and the potential to face the unexpected twists and turns we encounter. Every woman wants to love unconditionally, foster the best of friendships, express observations flawlessly, leave places that don't allow growth, stand for principles, mentor when asked, and allow closure when needed. But, we continue to remain imprisoned in our own thoughts, drowning in emotions many times.

Deep within us lies divinity waiting to be kindled — a fire that once lit can light up the path ahead. The Divine has walked on this earth as human, and every human can be divine. Kindle the fire with the belief that you can and were born to do it.

Live

In The Present.
Not in Past,
Not in Future

Life can indeed be overwhelming. We often find ourselves either dwelling on troubling events of the past or worrying about uncertainties of the future, neglecting the importance of the present moment. The constant bombardment of messages urging us to "create memories" or "protect the future" only adds to this challenge.

Our conditioning also plays a significant role. As parents, we often focus on our past experiences in hopes of securing a better future for our children. However, it's essential to shift our perspective and learn to live each day fully.

When you catch yourself drifting into thoughts of the past or future, take a pause. Breathe deeply, hydrate yourself, and become aware of your surroundings. By easing into the present moment, you can alleviate the burden of overthinking.

Trust in the universe and the energies around you. Remember that you are not alone in this journey; we co-create everything together. As a favorite quote from the movie Kung Fu Panda reminds us, "Yesterday is history, tomorrow is a mystery, today is a gift. That's why it's called the present."

Magic

Can Be Experienced Through Calm

Calm is the absence of strong emotions.

It's incredibly common for women to find themselves ensnared in a cycle of overthinking and planning. Even when appearing to be at rest, whether lying on a bed or sitting on a couch, their minds can be in a state of absolute frenzy.

As the week unfolds, deadlines loom, household chores await completion, and to-do lists continue to grow. Trapped in a false sense of relaxation, we exhaust our minds with incessant thoughts.

That's precisely why we need to embrace calmness. Calm is not just a state of being; it's a superpower.

It also holds magical powers. Here's what it can actually do as the mind quietens our creativity flows.

Calm works like a prism to a ray of light breaking it into a rainbow.

It helps to align. our thoughts to actions and break overthinking patterns. For one action there are thousands of thoughts. And sometimes that action may never take place.

Naturalize

Saying no, learning to Create Boundaries

One of the reasons women feel broken to pieces is because of lack of boundaries. We are not taught to say NO.

You get angry. Because your boundaries are not in place. Because you don't even know how to respond. Because it slowly becomes a comfort zone. Because abuse often wears a mask of love. Worst because you think bearing all this is probably ok.

But what those boundaries look like and how to know where exactly to place them?

So try the following:

Emotional Audit: Watch your emotions and if required journal everyday. What are you experiencing and why?

Self Assessment: Of your eating, sleeping and day to day activities. Each is influenced by emotions.

Identifying Triggers: What upsets you deeply? What makes you cry? What makes you angry? Who do you wish to avoid?

Self regulation: Eating on time, sleeping soundly and practicing mindfulness, seeking help when needed is key to regulation.

Boundaries can mean ...... Staying away or minimizing interaction with individuals who trigger or hurt.

Least engagement with them in conversations. Staying away from social media. Communicating clearly and firmly how and what affects you.

Boundaries protect you from turning into what hurts you.

O

Orchestrate

Your Victories Through Learnings

Failure.

Failure is one of the most painful experiences known to mankind. It's a knot in our minds, a pit in our stomachs, and an ache in our hearts. Despite beginning with dreams and intentions to excel, sometimes we falter. Our plans may have been robust, our goals well-designed, our actions focused, and our sacrifices immeasurable. Yet, failure remains a part of the human experience. The true test lies in how we respond to failure. Every setback offers an opportunity for growth and learning, paving the way for future success. To overcome failure, we must build our confidence by revisiting past victories, face ourselves with acceptance, and seek support from mentors if needed. By understanding the situation holistically and challenging our own beliefs, we can learn from failure and orchestrate our future wins.

List the dream, goals, plans, actions, and learnings from last failure. List resources, the support system and skill sets. And restart.

Failure is just an event We all are more than that.

It hurts, but all that's needed is to heal and move ahead!

Permit

Yourself to Rest without Guilt

The maximum growth that happens in the human body is during the first couple of years of life.

Isn't it amazing that infants sleep the most and maximum growth occurs during that time. Magic happens when both body and mind are at rest.

As we grow not only our sleeping hours decrease but the quality of sleep worsens.

We equate break with vacations or weekends.

Look at your body. Your eye blinks! And in that fraction of a second it rested. Your heart beats with pauses. The conscious brain has the power to push for rest every day, by making you sleep!! If you don't give it ... It forces a shutdown. People dozing in important meetings, drives ... We have endless examples.

It's sad we give less importance to rest.

It's sad we don't pay attention to the miracle and power of growth that it holds.

Rest is not just sleep. Rest is also focusing on one thing at a time and turning off other stimuli.

Focus on rest everyday. And you will be grateful to the body and mind responding back by increasing productivity and enhancing clarity!

Question

What Differentiates Average from the Great?

Great is something above average but we also equate it to immense effort and often unachievable.

What differentiates great from average?

Here are few traits that are easily replicable in our lives nudging us towards greatness in what we do and where we are:

1) Presence

Being in the moment fully. Be there. Mentally and emotionally. It's the most impactful act that makes the average great!

2) Punctuality

Show up on time. If you value time, time will value you. It's that simple. It's not about others being late. It's about you being on time.

3) Active listening

The most underrated yet powerful skill that can actually change the energy of the room is active listening. Listen to words, the emotions and the energy of the person talking to you.

4) Updating and learning new skills

If you are technically sound and updated in work, trust me you are great!!

Nothing beats a well skilled and knowledgeable person.

5) Mindfulness at home and work place

Every word and act have the power to impact people around you. Being mindful helps us cultivate the best of relationships.

Greatness is infectious!!

We all want to be great because it makes us feel good. What we forget is that it makes those around us feel good too!!

Responsibility

Of Your Happiness, Lies with You

We all want to be happy. It's that simple.

Each of us has our own definition and parameters for it.

Few things that make us happy are…

Love from parents, partner, children and siblings. Companionship from friends and colleagues. Money can also buy us a few things that bring happiness, allow us to travel to places and discover new cultures.

Well, it could be different for all ...

But honestly on whom does the responsibility of your happiness lie? And why is the world so sad today?

Even the happiest looking people, if given space, break down. There could be a lot of reasons that make us sad.

The primary reason is we DO NOT take responsibility for our own happiness!!

Honestly, each should keep this power to herself only.

Observe yourself over a period of time. And make a note of what truly brings you happiness. List everything out.

Have the wisdom of knowing things that lie in your control. One can alter that for personal joy. Navigate through your life in a way that brings happiness.

Talk to your loved ones about what brings joy to you. Much of our sadness is due to non-communication and silent expectations.

Stand

Up For Yourself

This is a poem written by me dedicated to all women reading this book I go back in time-

When I was a little girl
Dreams in my eyes of serving the world
In a room filled with books
I was my own knight and my own rook
Facing exams day after day
Making inroads paving my own way
My parents were my strength
My friends would calmly hear me vent
It was my battle field
My sword and my shield
It was my victory
My losses ...
Both I could deal with...
Years on no one has the power to dim my light
Let the winds blow hard I survive countless fights
I will reach out though to people Who has seen me grow
To dust my broken shield, sharpen my sword,
Fill my quiver and repair my bow
No matter what surrounds me now
I am still that little girl who believed in herself
Above all ...
No matter what I don't give up on myself

T

Tribe

Find One That Has Your Back

At any given time, we are with people.

Our family, friends or workplace colleagues

Whether we like it or not, realize it or not, the truth remains that their behavior, words and actions impact us at conscious as well as subconscious levels.

We cannot change people but we can make a conscious choice to listen to the right kind of individuals

So, who are the best people to be with?

1) The Inspired: People who fill you with ideas to be better and to do better. The creative lot. They stand out from the crowd and make you look at things differently

2) The Motivated: The go-getters. These set of people will give you every reason to pursue your dreams and even show how it is done.

3) The Open Minded: They bring acceptance in life. While everyone may judge you, these people accept and help you make best of situations and yourself

4) The Passionate: My favorite kind of people. Always driven by dreams and bigger pictures they show you what the world should look like and nothing deters them

5) The Grateful: They help you practice gratitude and acknowledge what you have to begin with. Even in sad moments they bring relief.

These should be a part of your real and virtual world. What you hear and read also matters

We are definitely known by the company we keep!!!!

U

Uniqueness

Tap into Your DNA

Look around. There are innumerable things telling you to be like someone else.

"Cloned generation" as I love calling it!

Externally the faces of many are so plasticised that it's difficult to recognise them over a period of time. They all look alike.

Work wise there is this unending rat race of replicating lifestyles. Social media bears the silent testimony to that.

Step back. Go and stand in front of the mirror. Look at yourself. On this planet you are one of your kind. The only one.

Look at your hands, specifically your thumb.

That thumb print is so unique. It's used to identify you. If a mere little segment of your body makes you stand out from the rest, imagine if you tap into the whole of you!

So, let's remind ourselves what makes us UNIQUE.

In any situation there is something that you offer that makes you stand out.

Never ever lose sight of that. Celebrate what you bring to the table.

Be yourself. Always. You have your trademark smile. Your own poise. Your own grace. Own it. Who are you? What makes you... well You?!

Show up who and what you are unapologetically. If you don't honestly, who will?

Don't forget the power you hold to change things just by being yourself.

Your silence can end arguments. Your words can change the rules!

Every second that passes by defines your life. By being unique you are adding value to that second that no one else can.

V

Visualize

The Bigger Picture, Instead of Daily Drama

What's the big picture you are looking at??

Health Wealth Fame Experiences

Acknowledgement

Nearly all what are goals fall into these categories

And no matter what we must not lose sight of bigger picture Let that be the driving force

And keeping that image in mind, grab EVERY SINGLE OPPORTUNITY that leads you to it.

Many times, our own limiting beliefs stop us from grabbing the opportunities and that leads to mental turmoil. Sometimes the picture is so blurred that we keep existing in a space where we can truly thrive...

If you are struggling to see the picture or understanding how to make the best of opportunities understand that you are very caught up in your own story

The awareness should be followed by visualization of what you actually want to see yourself as!

Identify and let go of limiting beliefs. The strengths that you carry come out, all guns blazing...

Because no matter what we all deserve our very own BIG PICTURE

Wander

But Don't Get Lost

At any given moment your mind is lost in thoughts

If you examine your thoughts, it's evident that many around the goals, dreams and aspirations.

Next promotion or job New/bigger home new car

Next vacation

While each is bound to dream and strive, it also means failing to acknowledge where your present lies

This very present for which you once probably gave everything So take a pause

Soak in the moment

This very job is the one I really prayed and worked for This house is my home right now

I can travel (Hello!! Remember lockdowns!!) The vacation I made too was so amazing

You just shifted from future that's consuming you to the present that's a gift You just changed desire into gratitude

And in moments you are already feeling happier and lighter So where are you wandering?

X

Xerox

The Most Confident Part of You Again and Again

There are days when you are supremely confident. Or a phase of life when you were.

The word confidence can resonate with us in either way. It often reminds us of our best victories. It has the power to bring something extraordinary and at the same time disappear like a dream if we fail.

Confidence can be a game changer for anyone.

While many are blessed with confidence as an inborn trait, do you know it's also a skill set that can be acquired, worked upon and replicated again and again! Just like a Xerox...

To begin with, dress the part. It does not have to be expensive or fancy. But it definitely has to be something that you are comfortable in and carry well and make you look presentable.

Your smile can be your signature. Unique as it is. It creates understanding. Scientifically smiling releases endorphins and serotonin that elevate your own mood.

Nothing can beat good preparation. Be technically thorough about your work. It's something only you can do. Excellence is built on technically sound foundations.

Make a list of achievements you have made and pin it on the wall. It will remind you how far you have come and boost you. Pin that fab picture on the wall.

Sometimes all we need is a Xerox of our best selves!

Y

Yearn

To Hear Your Own Voice

Women are often labeled as talkative.

But honestly have you heard yourself in true self

A voice that has been trying to convey the deepest of feelings. A voice that was probably scared.

A voice that was true.

A voice that is happy to be noticed.

A voice that's complaining "Why now?" A voice that quivers and shakes.

A voice that finally wants to be heard.

It will begin with uneasiness and an uncomfortable smile.

Sometimes before hearing the actual words there may be a sob, a cry or a complete breakdown

Then comes the calm. The honesty in the eyes. And the strength to finally word the feelings in the truest way.

It's overwhelming and exhilarating moment but it is the turning point.

In that moment, in that situation, and sometimes for life... Hear your voice as often as you can.

Zeal

For a Life that Truly is Yours

The pace at which life moves is unbelievable. Days may seem slow, but months pass by quickly, and years vanish in a blink of an eye. Often, we slip into our routines without paying attention to ourselves. There are recurring circumstances and uncomfortable situations that feel all too familiar, making us wonder, "Again?" It's crucial to spend time with yourself and conduct a self-assessment. Scan your body for signs of discomfort, such as a racing heart, faster breathing, loss of appetite, or sleep disturbances. Examine your predominant thoughts and emotions throughout the day. Identify what makes you happy, sad, excited, or angry. Assess your surroundings to determine where you feel most comfortable and where you do not. Commit to breaking patterns that no longer serve you. Believe in your ability to make positive changes, no matter how challenging it may seem. Recharge yourself daily through activities like exercise, meditation, and listening to music. Engage in positive self-talk, thoughts, and actions. Celebrate every achievement and pattern that you break. Kindness to yourself should become a habit. Remember, you have the power to change things that don't serve you. Let your state of mind be driven by purpose, energy, and relentless drive. May each of you always have a zest for life.

Know Your Author

I was born on the floor of a house in a little village in Bihar on 31/08/79.

Unvaccinated, I survived through the childhood years not succumbing to pneumonia, diarrhea etc. As a public health specialist can't help mentioning that!!

Interestingly I was raised in Goa. Talk about what destiny can possibly look like! That alone causes people to envy me! Jokes apart growing up in a multicultural environment was beautiful.

I grew up to be a doctor specializing in public health. I did return to Bihar to be part of the World Health Organisation lead immunisation program, and many other public health related projects over the years. Life came full circle.

Meanwhile, I nearly died twice: once in an agonizing electric shock and the other from bleeding postpartum during the birth of my second baby. There were many emotional upheavals, financial challenges, and career breaks too, as there would be with anyone reading this. So, this led me to become a Mindset Coach for women.

One thing I never give up is learning. I learned from joy and sorrow, I learned from others and myself, I learned from victories and failures, I learned from friends and enemies. NO MATTER WHAT, I CHOSE TO LEARN.

And the biggest learning is this: One day, everything makes sense, provided you learn. I feel grateful, joyous, and blessed. I am thankful to each of you for reading this. Wish you peace and loads of love.

Simmi

Coming Up Next

Let's Talk (Hear) about Women
Extraordinary Stories about Ordinary Women

Chapter 1

The Aunt/Poet

The dusty lanes from the tarred road led to an old mansion flanked by well-manicured fields on either side. It was the largest house in the village and today it seemed radiant with lights as the wedding was under way. The walls were adorned with a fresh coat of paint and decorated with beautiful motifs that were popular for the region. Below the paint though, the walls were old and they had witnessed 8 decades of stories silently.

The chatter, laughter and songs streamed in the corridors and the multiple rooms of that huge old mansion. In the largest room, that once housed the matriarch of the mansion. She had passed away years back, but her presence was still unmistakable. it felt as if she was still commanding presence, watching over the three generations that had gathered in this moment of time. In that very room sat a quiet figure draped in a pristine white saree. She seemed pious to all those around her. Old eyes full of love, wrinkled fingers rolling a pair of prayer beads and an angelic smile. There was conversation happening around her but she seemed oblivious. The first born of the matriarch loved respected and adored by the family radiated her grace.

Kanchan stood at the entrance, staring at her intensely for some minutes. This place felt hallowed, like a shrine, so she stepped barefoot to the old lady and bowed respectfully, touching her feet. The prayer beads stopped rolling, and the old lady clutched Kanchan's hand affectionately, her gaze traveling from face to hands again. The elderly lady questioned Kanchan, 'So, is this the hand that cures people?'

Then she gently tilted towards the wall and continued, 'When I was a little girl, education was a luxury and privilege, and it was difficult to step away from the homes. If fathers were kind, tutors would come and teach a few basic words.

As a little girl, I once tried writing something on a torn piece of paper and was reprimanded for the same. Back then, a stick on the palms was enough to break one's spirit, so well, it ended at that once and for all.'

Kanchan looked at those old hands intently, noticed a few ink stains, and could not resist asking her, 'Don't your hands have a different story to tell? No matter what, haven't you been battling and still learning to write?'

The old lady began to sing, and her voice filled the courtyard of the very home where she had sobbed as a child with hurt palms. The noise quietened in the staircase and in the halls slowly all the relatives began to assemble towards that one central room. The hand that was once reprimanded and stopped from writing had not given up at all. She had stood her ground and learned to write over the years and had written songs one after another having her own book of hymns dedicated to the gods who never listened to her prayers. Today she was singing melodiously to the same gods. Life had come to a full circle as the new generation of girls from this home were now highly educated.

The house, the family and the spirit of the matriarch just listened to the songs that were composed by this lady who was known just as the senior most aunt but was a poet.